I0813569

BIG FARM MACHINES

Maria Koran

EYEDISCOVER

Go to www.openlightbox.com and enter this book's unique code.

BOOK CODE

AVS76325

EYEDISCOVER brings you optic readalongs that support active learning.

Published by Lightbox Learning Inc.
276 5th Avenue, Suite 704 #917
New York, NY 10001
Website: www.openlightbox.com

Library of Congress Control Number: 2022935956

978-1-7911-4878-2 (hardcover)

Printed in Guangzhou, China
1 2 3 4 5 6 7 8 9 0 26 25 24 23 22

092022
102121

Project Coordinator: John Willis
Layout: Sushant Deshpande

The publisher acknowledges Getty Images and Shutterstock as the primary image suppliers for this title.

EYEDISCOVER provides enriched content, optimized for tablet use, that supplements and complements this book. EYEDISCOVER books strive to create inspired learning and engage young minds in a total learning experience.

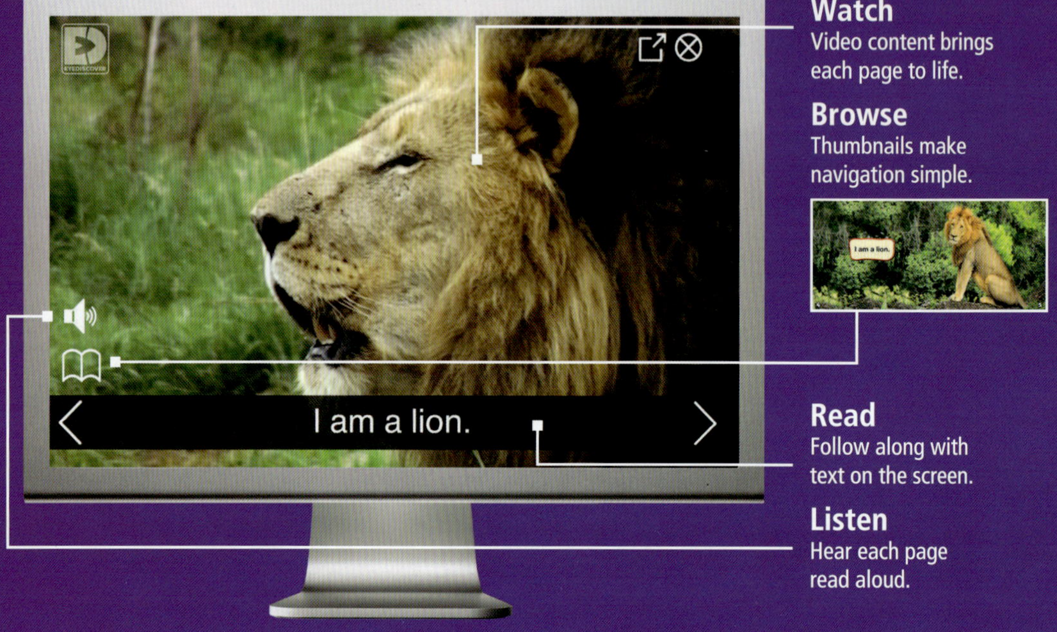

Watch
Video content brings each page to life.

Browse
Thumbnails make navigation simple.

Read
Follow along with text on the screen.

Listen
Hear each page read aloud.

Your EYEDISCOVER Optic Readalongs come alive with...

Audio
Listen to the entire book read aloud.

Video
High resolution videos turn each spread into an optic readalong.

OPTIMIZED FOR

- ✓ TABLETS
- ✓ WHITEBOARDS
- ✓ COMPUTERS
- ✓ AND MUCH MORE!

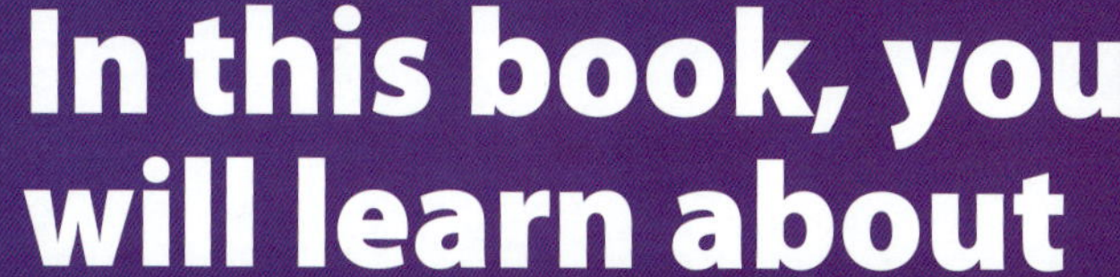

- what they are
- what they look like
- how they are used

and much more!

Farms are important around the world. They grow the food people need to eat.

9420R
JOHN DEERE

Tractors are some of the most important farm machines. Farmers put different tools on tractors to do jobs around the farm.

Tools on the front of tractors can help farmers move hay bales. Tools on the back can help farmers dig holes.

40
10

Other machines may be attached to tractors, too. Cultivators get fields ready for new crops to grow.

Once a field is ready, farmers need to plant seeds. Seeders help farmers spread seeds across a large area.

Farmers use large sprayers to control weeds. This helps protect their crops as they grow.

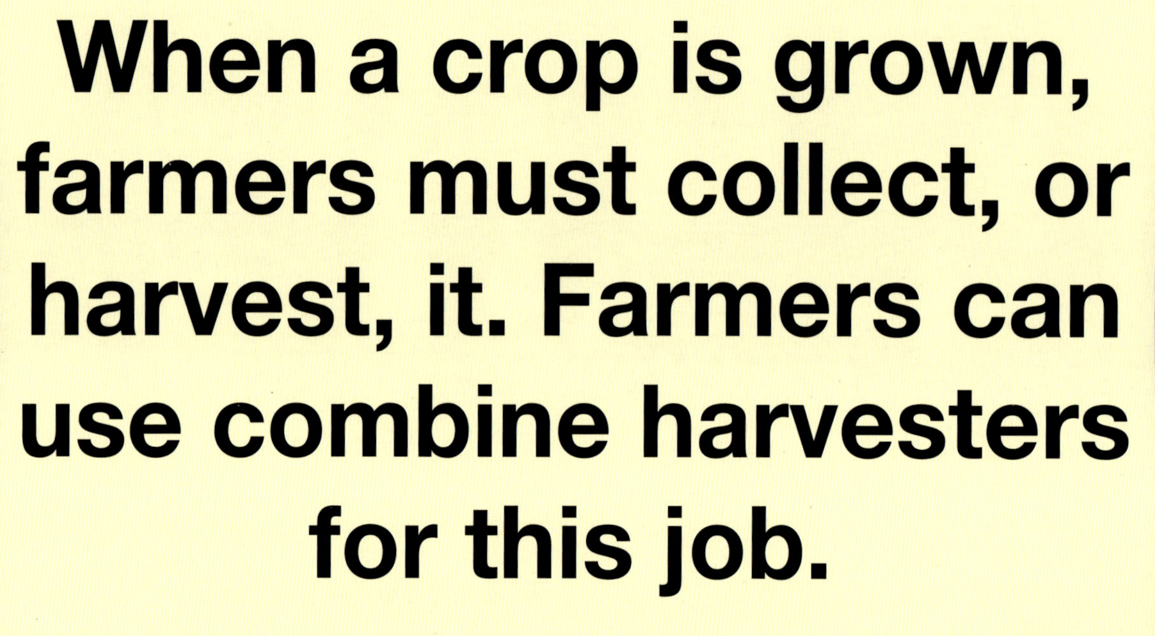

When a crop is grown, farmers must collect, or harvest, it. Farmers can use combine harvesters for this job.

Many farmers sell their harvested crops at markets. They often use pickup trucks to take the crops there.

The tools farmers use have changed over time. New machines help them grow more crops more easily.

BIG FARM MACHINES BY THE NUMBERS

The **first cultivators** were created in the **1800s**. They were **pulled** by **horses**.

The **seeder** was **invented** in **1701** by a man named **Jethro Tull**.

Depending on the **size**,
a **sprayer**
can cost between

$50 and **$10,000**.

The biggest
combine harvesters
can harvest more than
110 tons (100 metric tons)
of crops each hour.

PICKUP TRUCKS made up
5 of the top **10 best-selling vehicles**
in the **United States** in **2020**.

The **world's largest**
tractor is **27 feet** (8.2 meters) long.
It weighs more than **46 tons**
(42 metric tons).

KEY WORDS

Research has shown that as much as 65 percent of all written material published in English is made up of 300 words. These 300 words cannot be taught using pictures or learned by sounding them out. They must be recognized by sight. This book contains 55 common sight words to help young readers improve their reading fluency and comprehension. This book also teaches young readers several important content words, such as proper nouns. These words are paired with pictures to aid in learning and improve understanding.

Page	Sight Words First Appearance
4	are, around, eat, farms, food, grow, important, need, people, the, they, to, world
7	different, do, most, of, on, put, some
8	back, can, help, move
11	be, for, get, may, new, other, too
12	a, is, large, once, plant
15	as, their, this, use
16	it, must, or, when
19	at, many, often, take, there
20	changed, have, more, over, them, time

Page	Content Words First Appearance
7	farmers, jobs, machines, tools, tractors
8	hay bales, holes
11	crops, cultivators, fields
12	area, seeders, seeds
15	sprayers, weeds
16	combine harvesters
19	markets, pickup trucks

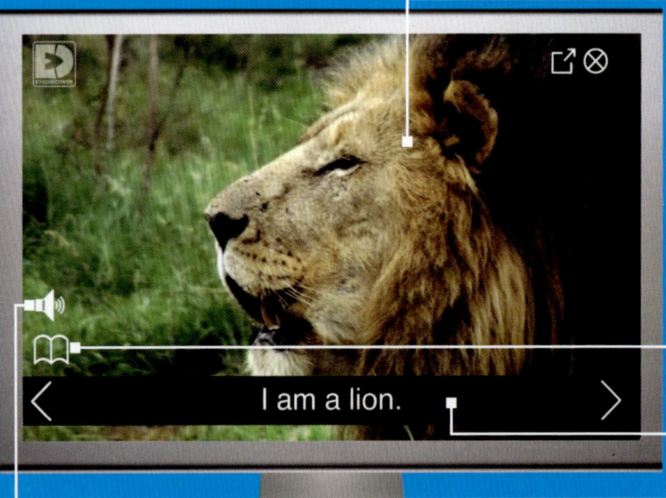

Watch
Video content brings each page to life.

Browse
Thumbnails make navigation simple.

Read
Follow along with text on the screen.

Listen
Hear each page read aloud.

Go to www.openlightbox.com and enter this book's unique code.

BOOK CODE

AVS76325